T0007947

SEASONS

A YEAR IN NATURE

by Hannah Pang

Illustrated by Clover Robin

360 degrees

For Nana and Grandpa, with whom I enjoyed many seasons,
and for Mia, who will learn all about them ~ H.P.

For Kev and Winnie x ~ C.R.

For nine years of seasons ~ N.B.

360 DEGREES, an imprint of Tiger Tales
5 River Road, Suite 128, Wilton, CT 06897
Published in the United States 2021
Originally published in Great Britain 2020
by Little Tiger Press Ltd.
Text by Hannah Pang
Text copyright © 2020 Little Tiger Press Ltd.
Illustrations copyright © 2020 Clover Robin
ISBN-13: 978-1-944530-37-2
ISBN-10: 1-944530-37-1
Printed in China • LT/1800/0274/0122
All rights reserved
2 4 6 8 10 9 7 5 3

www.tigertalesbooks.com

The Forest Stewardship Council® (FSC®) is an international,
non-governmental organization dedicated to promoting responsible
management of the world's forests. FSC® operates a system of forest
certification and product labeling that allows consumers to identify
wood and wood-based products from well-managed forests and other sources.

For more information about the FSC®, please visit their website at www.fsc.org

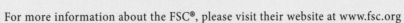

Nature is like a magical picture that changes with the seasons.

A mighty European oak stands lush and green
in summer but leafless and cold in winter.

The Arctic transforms from midnight Sun to
midday darkness, while the rivers of Alaska flow wildly
until freezing solid in the colder months.

At the bottom of the world, an Australian mangrove
teems with land animals one season, and fish the next.
And in China's Yellow Dragon Valley,
the colors change from white to green and gold.

Seasons bring drama all across the globe and nowhere more
than on the plains of the Kenyan Maasai Mara,
where battles of life and death are fought and won
in seasons wet and dry.

Open the pages of this innovative book
to discover the magic of nature . . . .

MIGHTY OAK

Just look at this beautiful **European oak tree** as it sprouts and sheds its **leafy coat**. All year through, the **mighty oak** gives food and shelter to the creatures that call it **home**.

SPRING

Watch the great oak burst into life with fresh, green leaves as the sweet sound of birdsong fills the meadow.

This **purple hairstreak caterpillar** needs to eat as much as possible before it can become a beautiful butterfly.

Many flowers, like **bluebells**, pop up in spring because of the warm sunshine. Buzzing **honeybees** bite a hole in the bottom of the flower to drink the sweet nectar.

The tree attracts many bugs, which hungry birds like to eat for lunch! But you might not see this **wood warbler**. It nests in the long grass, hidden from predators.

SUMMER

See the tree standing full and lush in the summer sun, with new chicks chirping for a juicy worm!

Butterflies flutter around the tree, looking to lay their eggs on leaves.

Most **rabbits** live underground in burrows, or rabbit holes, popping out to eat grass and other plants around the tree.

Green acorns grow in summer. They contain a single seed that may grow into a mighty new tree.

Unlike most other moths, this **hummingbird hawk-moth** is often out in the day and can even fly in the rain! It likes to sip on honeysuckle flowers.

AUTUMN

Now the leaves are turning gold and brown before falling to the ground. And the animals are busy stocking up on food before the winter comes.

This funny-looking mushroom has a funny-sounding name: the **chicken of the woods**! It likes to live on oak trees but can cause the tree to rot, or even make it collapse.

Red deer feed on the brown acorns that fall from the oak tree in autumn. They have brownish-gray coats now but red ones in the warmer months.

The best time to see or hear a **tawny owl** is on an autumn night, when the male and female owls call out to each other. Listen for their loud "hoo-hoo!"

Under the damp leaves, a bug battle is taking place! As night falls, the speedy **house centipede** captures all kinds of creepy-crawlies— from **worms** to **woodlice**.

WINTER

The tree is bare and the ground blanketed with snow. This season is a tough time for the animals. Most of them are hidden.

Badgers survive winter by living off the body fat they put on during their autumn feasting. They are active all year round but will stay underground if it gets too cold.

During the winter, the **hazel dormouse** hibernates inside a cozy woven nest. That means it goes into a deep sleep for many months without waking up!

Inside its special shelter called a chrysalis, this **caterpillar** is preparing for a major change: to become a beautiful butterfly!

Just like the dormouse, some **bats** also hibernate, often in old woodpecker holes. When they are deeply asleep, they barely breathe at all!

The **bumblebee** queen is the only bumblebee that will survive the winter. All her worker bees die, while she dozes safely in an underground hole until spring.

The tree stands still, but nature marches on. The mighty oak, and all the wildlife that live around it, change through every season in order to survive.

ARCTIC GLOW

At the **top**
of the Earth,
there's a place that's
very cold.
A world of **ice**
so **white**
in **winter**
that it takes
your breath away,
only to
melt again
with the **summer.**
Welcome to
the **Arctic!**

WINTER

The Sun hides for many months in winter. But the dazzling northern lights scatter across the sky!

A mother **polar bear** digs a deep den under the snow. Here she will give birth to her fluffy little cubs.

Long fingers of salty ice, called **brinicles**, can be found hanging beneath the frozen sea.

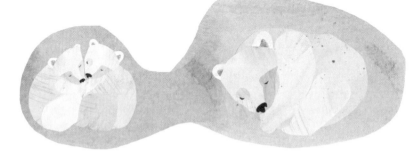

Like most seals, the **ringed seal** can survive the cold because it has a thick layer of body fat called blubber.

Narwhals are often called "unicorns of the sea." In winter, they like to swim in deep water underneath the thick ice.

SUMMER

The Sun is out and sparkling bright, but in the summer, it never sets. At the stroke of midnight, the Sun will still be blazing in the sky!

Every year, **snow geese** fly thousands of miles to settle in the Arctic. The long, warm summer days are perfect for raising chicks.

As the ice melts, **orcas** move into the open water to hunt for seals. They stay away from the ice in winter because it can injure their tall back fins.

The **musk ox** calf stays with its mother and often hides underneath her long, hairy "skirt" where it feels safe.

In summer, the **Arctic hare** and **Arctic fox** lose their white coats, which helped keep them hidden from predators in the snowy winter months.

The Arctic is a tough place for animals to live, and it's becoming even tougher. By taking care of our planet, we can help them to survive.

A WILD LAND

Alaska is bigger
and colder
than you could
ever imagine.
It rests high
above the sea,
where mountains
decorate the distance
and rivers flow
with fish.
Stand at the water's
edge and watch
the seasons change
before your eyes.

AUTUMN

The forest is ablaze with green and golden trees, while the ground is bathed in fire-colored weeds.

In autumn, **sandhill cranes** fly together in a V-shaped flock, heading south for winter.

With less salmon to eat, bears must fill up on other food before winter. Their autumn menu includes **pine nuts**, **berries**, and **leaves**.

During the autumn, male **Alaskan moose** fight to try and win the attention of a female moose.

WINTER

The frozen river winds an icy path between twiggy trees and green firs. Many animals are hidden, while those outside try to stay alive.

The **Alaskan moose** sheds its huge antlers in winter. New ones will begin to grow again in spring.

North American beavers are in their cozy lodge under the snow, snuggling up to keep warm. Their dam is close by.

The **wood frog**'s body turns to ice during the winter. When spring comes, it will thaw out before hopping away!

The **great horned owl** sets up home in an old eagle or squirrel nest, or sometimes a hole in a tree.

SPRING

Spring is a time for new beginnings. As rivers thaw, there is plenty of water for the wildlife, and pretty flowers sway among long, wavy grass.

Purple lupins are one of Alaska's first wildflowers to pop up in spring. Yellow poppies soon follow, where bumblebee queens sit to warm themselves.

Underwater, young **salmon** hatch. Then they leave the river and spend up to two years in a lake before swimming out to sea.

The **Canada lynx** looks for a mate in early spring. The female is pregnant for only a short while before giving birth to her kittens.

The **North American porcupine** is nocturnal, which means it only comes out at night. Its hard quills protect it against predators.

American minks also come out at night. Baby minks begin hunting at just eight weeks old but stay with their mom until autumn.

SUMMER

Fresh summer rain pitter-patters into the fast-flowing river. And with the summer comes salmon.

The **brown bears** of Alaska will spend most of the summer feasting on fish. Summer is a season of plenty!

The **four-spotted skimmer dragonfly** hovers like a helicopter, hunting other bugs in midair. Watch out, pesky mosquitoes!

Thousands of **red salmon** travel from the sea to the river where they hatched. Here they will lay their own eggs.

It's not just the bears that enjoy a fish dinner. Many birds, such as **eagles**, **ravens**, and **gulls**, wait patiently for any leftovers.

The **gray wolf** is not fussy and will eat most things, from moose to beavers. It even joins in for a bit of salmon fishing.

The **wolverine** is a greedy animal and will follow the wolf to scavenge on any uneaten food.

Fireweed is one of the first weeds to pop up after a forest fire, spreading its glorious colors across the ash.

Alaska gets more light in summer than winter. But even summer is pretty cold, making it a difficult place to live all year long.

WATER WONDERLAND

Let's make our way to a **boggy creek**, tucked away in **northern Australia**.

Here you will meet the **magical mangrove tree**, whose roots reach **far** and **wide**, **in** and **out** of the water.

DRY SEASON

The mangrove tree rests among a bed of wet mud during the dry season. The creek is drained of water, leaving a fishy feast behind.

Not far from the mangrove, the **swamp wallaby** spends the day resting, deep in the bush. The female wallaby carries her baby, or joey, in a pouch like a kangaroo.

The **striated heron** lives in or around the mangrove tree all year round. It likes to lurk among the roots, ready to pounce on a mudskipper or crab.

The **polished fiddler crab** looks like it's playing a violin as it waves its large claw from side to side. This warns off other males or attracts females.

A mommy **flying fox** protects her pup with her wings as she hangs from the tree. When nighttime falls, she will carry her pup in search of fruit.

With feet-like fins, the **barred mudskipper** is a fish that lives in water and on land! When two males meet, their top fins brighten as a warning sign.

Unlike many plants, the **red mangrove tree** can survive in or out of water, even salt water! During the dry season, it is dotted with small flowers.

WET SEASON

In the hot and steamy summer, pouring rains fill up the creek. Welcome to an underwater wonderland. But beware of all that lurks beneath!

A baby **mangrove red snapper** is more brightly colored than its parents. It stays in the mangrove nursery while the females go out to sea and lay their eggs.

With the snap of its large claw, the **pistol shrimp** makes a loud popping sound to scare off predators.

The **azure kingfisher** is a master at diving for fish. It watches from a low-hanging branch before swooping down to catch its prey.

Baby **mangrove monitor lizards** hatch during the wet season, when there are more insects to eat.

The **banded archerfish** shoots down insects from nearby branches with jets of water!

The **dugong**, or sea cow, can sometimes be spotted in channels near mangroves. It likes to graze on seagrass and is related to the elephant.

The mangrove is a challenging place to live. Animals and plants have to lead a double life in order to cope with the dramatic changes that take place in their home.

A PLACE OF MAGIC

In the Yellow Dragon Valley, glittering stone surrounds crystal blue ponds. Be **still** and **wait** on the mountainside to see some of China's rarest creatures.

WINTER

Wintertime is beautiful, with snow-dusted trees, frozen ground, and monkeys huddling to keep warm.

You'll only see the **Pallas's cat** after dusk, when it comes out to hunt for small rodents and birds. It grows a long, fluffy coat in winter to keep warm.

Sichuan golden snub-nosed monkeys survive the winter because of their thick fur and flat snub noses, which would get frostbitten if they were too long!

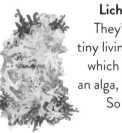

Lichens are not plants. They're made up of two tiny living things: a fungus, which gathers water, and an alga, which makes food. So they are more like very good friends!

SPRING

Behind a fringe of golden catkins, sunshine sprinkles over the melting ponds. It is time for the moon bear to say hello to spring.

The brightly colored **Chinese monal** whistles and bobs up and down to attract a female's attention.

Himalayan birch catkins appear on the birch tree in spring. These pollen heads can sometimes grow more than 4.5 inches (11 cm) long!

The **red panda** can mostly be seen at night. It has sharp claws and a long tail for climbing up tall trees, away from predators. Like many animals in the valley, it feeds mainly on **bamboo shoots**.

SUMMER

Summer brings the sunshine but also short showers of rain, leaving behind a land that's lush and green.

At this time of year, many animals, like the **blue sheep**, climb the steep mountain slopes to feed on fresh grass in the alpine meadows.

Wallcreepers nest in gaps between the rocks farther up the mountain.

The **Sichuan takin** has oily, rainproof fur to protect it from the summer rains.

Lady-slipper orchids might look delicate, yet they survive through the harshest winters, and on the very highest mountains, to reach full bloom in summer.

Not too far from the Yellow Dragon Valley, the **snow leopard** can be found. It uses its long tail to balance, leaping huge distances across the rocks.

The **Chinese peacock butterfly** has patterns that look like eyes. These scare away any animals that might try to eat it.

AUTUMN

The Yellow Dragon Valley is at its most beautiful in the autumn, when this magical place is filled with color and life.

The **giant panda** is an extremely rare animal that spends its time in the bamboo forests lower down the mountain. The mothers give birth to cubs that are so small, they could fit in your hand.

The **yellow-throated marten** likes to feed on **Sargent's rowan berries**, as well as squirrels, hares, rats, birds, insects, and even small deer!

Giant panda poop is green! This is because pandas mostly eat bamboo.

The **dwarf musk deer** is an excellent tree climber. Males have extremely long canine teeth, which they use to fight with other male musk deer.

The **Chinese pheasant** is a clumsy flier. It prefers to spend its time on the ground, feeding on leaves and insects.

After the summer rains, the **waterfalls** in the valley are now full and flowing. If you're lucky, you might see a panda playing in one!

The **northern hog badger** gets its name from its pig-like snout, which it uses to sniff out autumn fruit.

This land of golden rock and jewel-like ponds holds many rare and precious treasures in need of care.

LET IT RAIN

The grasslands
of the Kenyan
Maasai Mara
stretch as far
as the eye can see.

These ever-changing
plains bring life
to millions of
incredible creatures,
including an
army of
hungry predators!

DRY SEASON

Behind giant dust clouds and swirling water, the Great Migration is taking place across the Mara River. The animals have to get to the other side, or they will starve.

Blue wildebeest prefer short grass, so they often travel with zebras who nibble the grasses for them!

With its spotted coat, the **leopard** stays well hidden in a tree, ready to pounce on any animals below.

While animals gather under the **umbrella acacia** to keep cool, their poop and pee feed the tree!

With more than 60 sharp teeth, the **Nile crocodile** is a deadly hunter and as long as a car.

During the day, the **hippopotamus** cools down in the water. But beware: its yawn is a sign that it is angry!

WET SEASON

Dark clouds blanket the sky, and fresh grass grows on the plains beyond the river as the rains revive the wildlife all around.

The **ostrich** is the largest, heaviest bird in the world. It cannot fly, but it has very powerful legs and a kick deadly enough to kill a lion!

The **black-necked spitting cobra** is an angry snake. It will spit venom into the eyes of anything that scares it.

Sadly, there are very few **black rhinoceroses** left in the world, so you're unlikely to see one here. A baby black rhino will stay with its mother for up to three years.

Vlei ink flowers spring up after the rains.

Dung beetles roll up animal poop into balls, then bury them under the ground with their eggs inside.

These flowers are a tasty treat for **olive baboons**.

The Great Migration is one of the most dramatic events on Earth. For the animals, it is a journey of life and death.

From the **Arctic** tundra
to the **African** plains,
the changing of the **seasons**
keeps every **creature** and
plant working together
in **perfect balance**.
The **seasons** drive the
everlasting cycle that powers
all life on Earth.